The DLM Early Childhood EXPRESS

Ada, Once Again!

Written by Ana Nuncio

Illustrated by Luciana Powell

McGraw Hill **Wright Group**

The **McGraw·Hill** Companies

Illustrations:
The McGraw-Hill Companies, Inc./Luciana Powell

www.WrightGroup.com

 **Wright Group**

Printed in Mexico.

Send all inquiries to:
Wright Group/McGraw-Hill
P.O. Box 812960
Chicago, IL 60681

ISBN 978-0-07-658168-9
MHID 0-07-658168-3

4 5 6 7 8 9 DRN 16 15 14 13 12 11

There hangs Ada, sad as can be.

4

She's a plastic bag stuck in a tree.

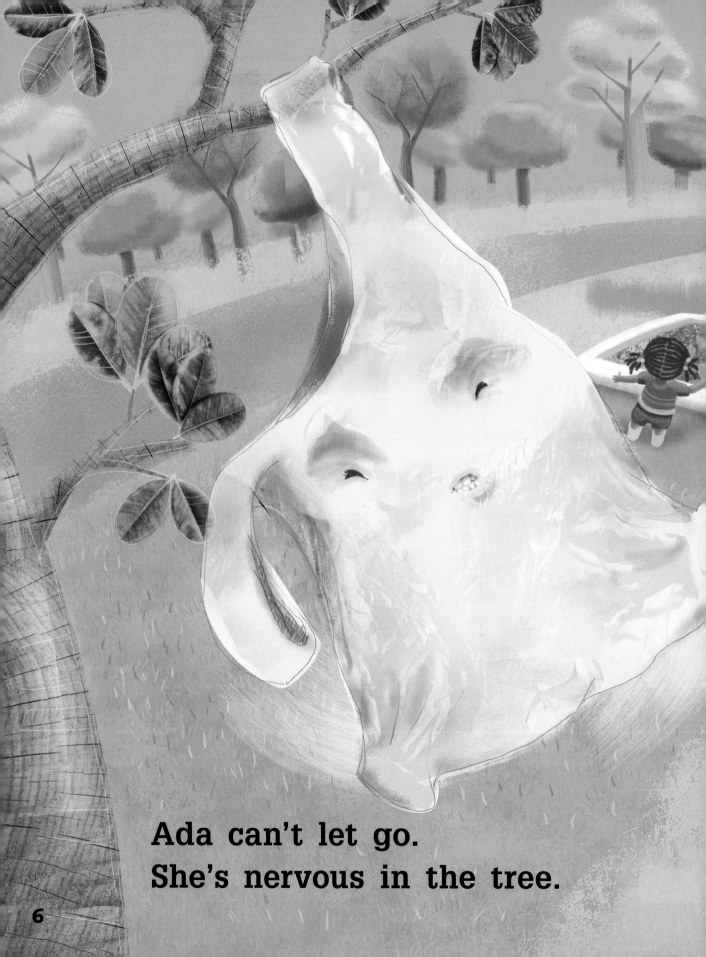

Ada can't let go.
She's nervous in the tree.

She looks down and sighs,
"That is where I should be."

Ada kicks and shouts,
"This is NOT where I belong!

No one sees me! No one listens!"
On her face a teardrop glistens...

Then crawling along the branch,
comes Paquita Ladybug so tiny,
in her cape all red and shiny.

Paquita says to Ada tenderly,

"If those children help, you'll get
to where you need to be.

"They love the Earth;
they'll know what to do.

Let's ask the wind
to blow for you, too."

Very hard the wind blows in,
and Ada begins to spin.

She spins to her left;
she spins to her right.

She'll get free with a bit of a fight!

"Let go and fly!"
A boy shouts up.
"Come on! We're ready!
Give it a try!"

20

Ada pulls and shakes,
wiggles and quakes.

Wait! Ada needs your help!

Yes, you know where Ada's place is,
the place where she belongs.

Recycling Center

PLASTIC
BAGS

Glass

METAL

Down falls Ada, ready to land.
She floats right toward
your waiting hand.

Pick her up, swoop her in,
place her in the recycling bin!

A new life waits for Ada,
happy, fantastic!
She'll be something else
made of plastic!

Ada says, "For now, good-bye to you.
But I'll soon be back as something
new!"

**Thoughts of a plastic bag:
Things I can be...**

a flowerpot
a plastic bottle
a bike helmet
...and a chair in your classroom!